CH

P9-ELG-339

SEP 2013

THE **MAGNA CARTA**

CORNERSTONE OF
THE CONSTITUTION

Roberta Baxter

Heinemann
LIBRARY

Chicago, Illinois

www.capstonepub.com
Visit our website to find out more information about Heinemann-Raintree books.

To order:
☎ Phone 800-747-4992
🖥 Visit www.capstonepub.com
to browse our catalog and order online.

© 2013 Heinemann Library

an imprint of Capstone Global Library, LLC

Chicago, Illinois

Edited by Abby Colich, Megan Cotugno, and Laura Hensley
Designed by Cynthia Della-Rovere
Original illustrations © Capstone Global Library Limited 2011
Illustrated by Oxford Designers & Illustrators
Picture research by Tracy Cummins
Originated by Capstone Global Library Limited
Printed and bound in the United States of America in North Mankato, MN. 012013 007120RP

16 15 14 13
10 9 8 7 6 5 4 3 2

Library of Congress Cataloging-in-Publication Data
Baxter, Roberta, 1952-
  The Magna Carta : cornerstone of the Constitution / Roberta Baxter.
      p. cm.—(Documenting U.S. history)
  Includes bibliographical references and index.
  ISBN 978-1-4329-6756-7 (hbk.)—ISBN 978-1-4329-6765-9 (pbk.) 1. Magna Carta—Juvenile literature. 2. Constitutional history—Great Britain—Juvenile literature. 3. Great Britain—History—John, 1199-1216—Juvenile literature. I. Title.
  JN147.B39 2012
  342.03'3—dc23   2011037932

Acknowledgments
The author and publishers are grateful to the following for permission to reproduce copyright material:akg-images: pp. 15, 17; Alamy: pp. 5 (© Alistair Laming), 8 (© World History Archive), 18 (© Homer Sykes); Bridgeman p. 34 (Peter Newark American Pictures); Corbis: pp. 6 (© Justin Lane/epa), 12 bottom (© Ric Ergenbright), 12 top (© Heritage Images), 14 (© Bettmann), 22 (© Stapleton Collection), 27 (© Stapleton Collection), 33 (© Bettmann); Getty Images: pp. 11 (Hulton Archive), 19 (The Bridgeman Art Library/Italian School), 28 (JANE MINGAY/AFP), 35 (James Sharples), 36 (MPI), 39 (KAREN BLEIER/AFP), 40 (Matt Cardy); istockphoto: pp. 25 (© Georgios Kollidas), 42 (© Dave Long); Library of Congress Rare Book Division Washington: pp. 30, 32; National Archives: p. 7; Shutterstock: pp. 24 (© Rui Saraiva), 26 (© Filip Fuxa), 43 (© Adrio Communications Ltd); The Granger Collection, NYC: p. 20.

Cover image of the Magna Carta reproduced with permission from Corbis (© Joshua Lott/Reuters). Cover image of King John signing the Magna Carta reproduced with permission from Corbis (© Stapleton Collection).

Every effort has been made to contact copyright holders of material reproduced in this book. Any omissions will be rectified in subsequent printings if notice is given to the publisher.

Contents

Some words are printed in bold, **like this**. You can find out what they mean by looking in the glossary.

Important Documents

The best way to understand the past is to read the words of the people who lived in that time. Letters, newspapers, books, and official documents that survive tell us the story of how the people lived, what they thought, and what they hoped for.

Two kinds of sources

There are two kinds of historical records: **primary sources** and **secondary sources**. We need both to truly understand historical events.

Primary sources are documents written during a certain time period. Letters, diaries, newspapers, and official government documents are primary sources. These eyewitness accounts give us a feel for the past—even if it was hundreds of years ago.

Secondary sources are written from primary sources. People will collect information from primary sources and write a new book or **article** about the events. The new written materials, such as this book, are secondary sources.

The Magna Carta

An important ancient primary source is the Magna Carta, written nearly 800 years ago in England. The Magna Carta said that even the king was not above the law, and that he must respect the rights of others.

The original Magna Carta was written in **Latin**, the official language of the Catholic Church in that period. Latin was also the language of educated people. Soon after the king approved the Magna Carta, it was translated into French and English. County courts across England had the document read out loud. That way, even people who could not read would hear and understand the words.

Two copies of the 1215 Magna Carta are displayed today inside the British Library in London, England.

Liberties for the people

The Magna Carta was an agreement between England's King John and wealthy landowners called **barons**. In the 1200s, people feared that powerful kings would become **tyrants** and use their power against the people. The Magna Carta proclaimed that even the king had to follow the law. It also established basic rights that people could expect for themselves. It was the first time that an English king had been forced to proclaim **liberties** for people under his rule.

It took more than the writing of the Magna Carta in 1215 to ensure the freedoms of all people. The Magna Carta document had to be signed by different kings before the freedoms listed in it were considered part of the law of the land. Eventually, the freedoms extended beyond wealthy barons to everyday people.

The Magna Carta was written in 1215.

To America

The principles of the Magna Carta crossed the Atlantic Ocean with the earliest English **colonists** who settled in North America. These people had come to understand their basic rights under the Magna Carta in England. When they became colonists and had these rights violated by England, this led to the **Revolutionary War** (1775–1783).

The Magna Carta was written hundreds of years before the **Declaration of Independence** and the U.S. **Constitution**. But the writers of these newer documents used ideas from the Magna Carta. Its ideas about freedom helped shape the law and government of the United States.

The U.S. Constitution is on display in the National Archives in Washington, D.C.

England in the Middle Ages

What was happening in the world when the Magna Carta was written in 1215? The powerful leader Genghis Khan captured and controlled most of China and Central Asia. He had one of the largest kingdoms ever known. England was one of many kingdoms that existed in what is now called Europe. The Americas were unknown to Europeans at the time. But both North and South America were full of thriving villages and cities.

Growing economy

In England economic growth brought changes to people's lives. Most people still worked in farming, but looms and the spinning wheel increased the production of cloth. Windmills and clocks were invented. Farmers and businessmen could use better roads and carts to transport their goods to other parts of the country. This was important as the population (the total number of people) and trade increased. The first English universities were started, and huge churches called cathedrals were built.

Many people were needed to support the household of a baron.

English system

The governing system of England was based on the king, **barons**, and **knights** (see the chart). The king allowed powerful men known as barons to lease (use) land that belonged to him. They had to swear loyalty to the king and also supply knights to fight for him. Knights were given land from the barons in payment for fighting for the baron and the king.

At the bottom of this system were the **serfs**. They did not own any land, but they worked the land for the barons and paid taxes to them. They were not free to leave the land. They even had to receive permission from the knight or baron to marry.

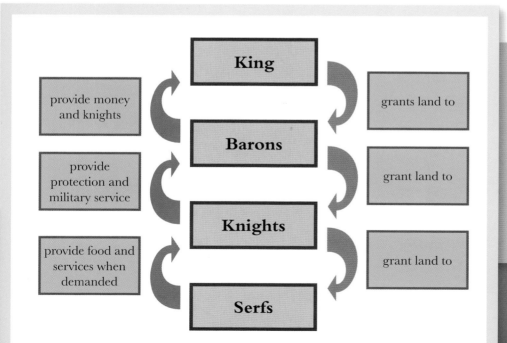

The system of society depended on the king, barons, knights, and serfs.

Charter of Liberties

A series of events led to the Magna Carta. More than 100 years before it was signed, King Henry I was crowned king of England in 1100. He proclaimed some freedoms in a document called the **Charter of Liberties**. This **charter** was issued to prevent the abuses that earlier kings had made against the Catholic Church and **nobles**.

Under earlier kings, when a baron died, his family had to buy the family's land again from the king. Church property had to be paid for again when a **bishop** died. If a daughter of a baron wanted to marry, the father had to pay the king. These payments raised money for the king. But the barons, knights, and Catholic Church resented having to pay them.

The Charter of Liberties was supposed to prevent the king from abusing the people. But most kings ignored the charter and charged fees and taxes as they wanted. However, the idea of the Charter of Liberties led to the development of the Magna Carta more than 100 years later.

"If any baron or earl of mine shall die, his heirs [family members] shall not be forced to purchase their inheritance [the money they receive from a family member], but shall retrieve it through force of law and custom."

—*Charter of Liberties*

King Henry I was crowned in 1100.

King Henry I improved the law and living conditions of the English people. But he did not obey the terms of the Charter of Liberties. He continued to charge people high taxes and to take land when he wanted it. Barons had no legal protection for their property. When King Henry I died, war erupted over who should be king. England was in a lawless state for years.

1100
King Henry I approves
the Charter of Liberties.

King Henry II

In 1154 a grandson of Henry I was crowned King Henry II. He married Eleanor of Aquitaine. Eleanor was from a section of France that was in Henry II's kingdom. Henry II and Eleanor grew up in France and lived there as much as they lived in England.

Henry II and Thomas Becket were friends before they became enemies.

Thomas Becket
(1118–1170)

Thomas Becket was the **archbishop** of Canterbury, a high-ranking official of the Catholic Church. He disagreed with Henry II about the Church obeying the king's laws. After his murder, the Catholic Church declared him a saint, or holy person.

1154
King Henry II is crowned. He goes on to enact changes that strengthen the property rights of nobles and the powers of judges in courts.

Henry II expanded the power of the royal government. Some of his changes helped the nobles. For example, he established property rights. He also gave more power to the judges who decided cases of law. His system led nobles to see the law and the court system as something that protected their property and made them stronger.

King Henry II had a battle with the Catholic Church over whether or not churchmen had to obey the king and the law. King Henry II, in an angry mood, said, "Will no one rid me of this turbulent [trouble-causing] priest?" Four knights heard his words and took action. They went to Canterbury Cathedral and killed Thomas Becket, the highest-ranking official in the Catholic Church in England (see the box).

1170
Thomas Becket is murdered. He had questioned whether the Church had to answer to the king.

Richard and John

Starting in 1095, the **pope** of the Catholic Church had asked **knights** to reclaim the holy city of Jerusalem from the Muslims (people who follow the religion of Islam). These efforts were called the Crusades. Groups of Christian knights traveled to Jerusalem and fought in bloody battles for the Catholic Church.

At the time of the Crusades, the Catholic Church was the most powerful organization in Europe. The influence of the pope reached across country lines, and his word was considered law in most of Europe. His law even overruled the law of the king in most countries.

The knights of the Crusades used complex weaponry in their battle for Jerusalem.

1189
King Henry II dies.
Richard I is crowned.

1189–1194
While King Richard is on a Crusade, his brother John rebels against him.

Richard the Lionhearted

When King Henry II died in 1189, his third son, Richard, was crowned king of England. He declared his intention to go on a Crusade. He swore to stop his sinful ways and become a soldier for the pope. Richard was already called Richard the Lionhearted for his military skill.

While King Richard I was on a Crusade, his brother John tried to become king. Richard forgave him for his rebellion. But while fighting in France, Richard was struck by an arrow and died from the wound.

Know It!

The rivalry between Richard and John led to stories, including that of Robin Hood and his Merry Men, who "robbed the rich and gave to the poor." We don't know if there really was a Robin Hood. The stories were told more than 100 years after the lives of John and Richard. But the conditions that Robin was said to fight against—including the abuses of the most powerful people—did exist.

King Richard the Lionhearted fought in a Crusade.

15

Only surviving son

After King Richard I died, John was the only surviving son of King Henry II and Eleanor of Aquitaine. He was known as John Lackland, because he was not expected to inherit (receive when someone dies) much land. He was also called John Softsword, because he was not often victorious in battle.

King John

John was crowned king of England on April 6, 1199. King John had some good qualities. He promised to accept the idea of property rights, as established under Henry II. He increased the power of the royal courts and tried to improve the system of laws in the country.

But King John was famous for his temper. When he was angry with **barons**, he would demand the taxes they owed. If they did not pay, King John took their castles. He raised the fees paid when a person married, inherited land, got a position as a sheriff or government official, or became a widow (woman whose husband died).

1199
King Richard I dies. King John becomes king.

Like the kings before him, John believed that he ruled because God made him the king. In his mind, this gave him all power over the barons and the people. As he set higher taxes and made more rules for the barons to obey, they began to think about rebelling against him. Whenever he heard about a possible rebellion, he threw those he suspected into prison. This would lead to many problems throughout his time as king—and would eventually lead to the Magna Carta.

John became king of England in 1199.

Powerful Church

During this period, the Catholic Church had tremendous power over the kings and people of England. The pope had to approve the king's marriage and give permission before a king went to war. The pope expected obedience.

Defying the Church

In 1205 the **archbishop** of Canterbury died. The **monks** of Canterbury Cathedral were to elect a new one. The king and the pope then had to approve these selections. King John had a person he wanted the monks to elect as archbishop. But the monks had their own person in mind. Both sides sent someone to Rome to be approved by Pope Innocent III.

The pope was upset by the disagreement between King John and the monks. So he chose another person, Stephen Langton (see the box). The monks agreed, but the choice made King John angry. He refused to let Langton into England.

Stephen Langton (1176–1228)

Stephen Langton was born in England and studied and taught in Paris, France. He became a Catholic priest and later a high-ranking church official. Eventually he was allowed to be the archbishop of Canterbury. He went on to advise King John to sign the Magna Carta.

1205
The archbishop of Canterbury dies. Disagreement about his replacement occurs.

Pope Innocent III was head of the Catholic Church.

The pope's interdict

As punishment, the pope declared an **interdict** on England in 1208. The interdict meant that there would be no church services, no sacraments (special holy ceremonies), and no marriages. The church officials could only christen infants (officially make them enter the Catholic Church) and hear the confessions of sins of dying people.

1208
The pope declares an interdict against England, as punishment for King John's refusal to obey the wishes of the Church.

King John taxes and loses battles

King John wanted to regain land he had lost in France. He thought this would bring more money to England. To raise money for a war against France, he began to tax the people even more. He decided he needed the pope's approval to do this, so he submitted to the pope's authority. He also agreed to send money to the Church every year. From then on, the pope supported John.

King John at first had some victories in France. But he was eventually defeated and had to pay more money to the French. The loss of money left the king with few resources. So King John raised taxes again. The barons were angry with the king's treatment of them. In November 1214, many of them pretended to meet for religious purposes. But instead, they discussed what to do about King John.

English knights fought for the king and the barons, including in the war against France.

1212
King John begins preparations for a war against France, in the hope of gaining land. When he loses, he raises taxes to help pay for the costs of the wars.

Barons' rights

In early 1215, a group of barons appeared before King John. They insisted that he restore their rights as he had promised to do when he was crowned (see page 16). King John was furious. But he said he would let them know his answer just after Easter.

For the next few months, both the king and the barons were preparing their castles for war and gathering supplies. They knew they might be fighting soon.

Fighting for Liberties

"…they all swore on the great altar that, if the king refused to grant these **liberties** and laws, they themselves would withdraw from their allegiance [loyalty] to him, and make war on him, til he should, by a **charter** under his own seal, confirm to them every thing they required…"

—*Roger of Wendover, historian from this era*

1213
The pope removes the interdict against England.

1214
The barons gather to discuss the high taxes that King John has imposed.

Rights at Runnymede

Battles between the king and the **barons** began. But in early June 1215, King John agreed to meet with the barons at Runnymede, a meadow about halfway between London and Windsor Castle, where King John often lived.

Magna Carta sealed

After several days of discussions, on June 15, King John agreed to the barons' demands. This agreement would become the Magna Carta. The 63 **articles** of the Magna Carta were written on **parchment** (animal skin that has been dried). The words are in **Latin**. King John placed his seal on the parchment, showing his agreement.

King John puts his seal on the Magna Carta.

1214–1215
King John and the barons fight battles against each other's forces.

In the Magna Carta, King John promised several things, including the following:

- He would not interfere with the Catholic Church.

- The king cannot impose taxes without approval.

- The cities and villages could elect their own officials and carry out city business.

- A group of barons would be chosen to make sure the rule of law was followed.

- The king would choose court officials who understood and would obey the law.

- A person accused of a crime must have a fair trial.

- A person can only be put in prison after legal judgment by his peers or by the law of the land.

- A free man cannot be imprisoned or have his possessions taken away from him unfairly.

It was the first time that a king accepted limits on his powers. He said that he and all future kings must act within the rule of law.

June 1215
The two sides meet at Runnymede. The Magna Carta is written and sealed.

No peace

The Magna Carta was meant to bring peace between King John and the barons. But John did not want to give up so much power. So within a few months, he acted against its terms. Both sides returned to war.

The rebel barons had taken over an important stronghold called Rochester Castle. King John surrounded and attacked Rochester Castle and stayed there for seven weeks. He finally captured the fortress in November. The barons also attacked castles owned by King John.

Rochester Castle was recaptured by King John and his knights.

Know It!

Magna Carta means the "Great **Charter**." The document got this name because of its size and importance.

1215–1216
The forces of King John and the barons fight again.

Then, King John led his **knights** to fight against an invasion by the French king. But many of the barons refused to fight with him.

King Henry III

In October 1216, King John became ill and died. Before his death, he named his young son king. He would be known as King Henry III.

King Henry III became king when he was only nine years old. An adviser, William Marshall, carried out the business of the kingdom until Henry was old enough to make decisions himself. In 1225 Henry III reconfirmed the Magna Carta. He became full king in 1234.

"No free man shall be seized or imprisoned, or stripped of his rights or possessions…"

—*Magna Carta*

Henry III reconfirmed the Magna Carta in 1225.

October 1216
King John dies. Henry III is crowned king.

1225
King Henry III reconfirms the Magna Carta.

1234
Henry III becomes full king.

Influence of the Magna Carta in Great Britain

Through the years, different experts interpreted the Magna Carta. It became thought of as a basis for English **common law**, which is the foundation for the legal system in England today.

Creating Parliament

One of the **clauses** of the Magna Carta (see the box on top of page 27) created a group of important people who would help run the kingdom. These people would be chosen by the **barons**. This was an important step in the establishment of the English **Parliament**, which is at the heart of British lawmaking today.

Parliament meets at the Palace of Westminster, shown here, in London, England.

1590s–1620s
Edward Coke interprets and writes about the Magna Carta. His writings inspire the common people to seek more rights under the law.

Rights for all

The Magna Carta did not ensure the rights of the common English people. Rather, the terms proclaimed the rights of the wealthy barons. But as time went on, the ideas became popular with common people, too. Ordinary people came to believe that they deserved these same rights. The writings of Edward Coke (see the box) led the common people to campaign for their rights.

"…that the barons choose five-and-twenty barons of the kingdom…who shall be bound with all their might, to observe and hold, and cause to be observed, the peace and **liberties** we have granted and confirmed to them by this our present **Charter**…"

—*Magna Carta*

Edward Coke
(1552–1634)

Edward Coke argued that even kings had to obey common law. He helped write the Petition of Right, which established legal principles based on the Magna Carta. Among these principles was the idea that only Parliament could impose taxes. He also argued that a person has the right to know what crime he is charged with. Coke's writings and rulings on cases established English common law.

The British government

Many aspects of the Magna Carta have influenced British government. Three specific clauses of the Magna Carta are part of English law today.

Clause 1

Clause 1 established the freedom of the English Church. It reads as follows:

> FIRST, We have granted to God, and by this our present Charter have confirmed, for Us and our Heirs [family members] for ever, that the Church of England shall be free, and shall have all her whole Rights and Liberties inviolable [incapable of being taken away]. We have granted also, and given to all the Freemen of our Realm, for Us and our Heirs for ever, these Liberties under-written, to have and to hold to them and their Heirs, of Us and our Heirs for ever.

English law today protects rights for everyone.

28

Clause 9

Clause 9 established the "ancient liberties" for the city of
London. The city could elect its own officials and carry out city
business. It reads as follows:

> THE City of London shall have all the old Liberties and
> Customs which it hath been used to have. Moreover We
> will and grant, that all other Cities, Boroughs, Towns,
> and the Barons of the Five Ports, as with all other Ports,
> shall have all their Liberties and free Customs.

Clause 29

Clause 29 established that people can expect basic rights if they
are accused of a crime and must go to trial. It reads as follows:

> NO Freeman shall be taken or imprisoned, or be
> disseised [dispossessed or deprived] of his Freehold, or
> Liberties, or free Customs, or be outlawed, or exiled, or
> any other wise destroyed; nor will We not pass upon him,
> nor condemn him, but by lawful judgment of his Peers,
> or by the Law of the land. We will sell to no man, we will
> not deny or defer to any man either Justice or Right.

Influence of the Magna Carta in the United States

At the same time that Edward Coke was writing about the Magna Carta in England, the American **colonies** began to develop.

People left England to establish communities in North America for a variety of reasons, such as freedom to practice their religion freely.

Colonial charters

The colonies were set up under the leadership of the king and the English **Parliament**. Each colony had its own set of laws, listed in **charters** for the king to sign.

The early American colonists brought English law with them.

Edward Coke wrote most of the Virginia Charter for the colony of Virginia. He wrote that the **colonists** would have the "**liberties**, franchises [authorities] and immunities [protections of rights]" of English citizens.

1607
Jamestown is settled under the Virginia Charter.

1620
Plymouth Colony is started.

1629
A charter is given for the Massachusetts Bay Colony.

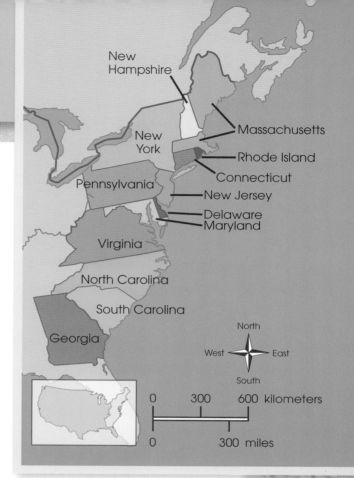

This map shows the first 13 colonies established in America.

Similarly, the charter for the Massachusetts Bay Colony stated that people would "have and enjoy all liberties and immunities of free and natural subjects [citizens]." Many of these words matched almost exactly the words of the Magna Carta.

In 1687 William Penn, founder of Pennsylvania Colony, published a pamphlet called *The Excellent Privilege of Liberty and Property: Being the Birth-Right of the Free-Born Subjects of England.* In it he included a copy of the Magna Carta. Penn's plan of government for the colony included freedom of religion, freedom from unjust imprisonment, a jury system, and amendments (changes to the laws). These were all ideas from the Magna Carta.

1687
William Penn writes *The Excellent Privilege of Liberty and Property*, which includes the first printed copy of the Magna Carta in North America.

Taxes are imposed

In the period before the **Revolutionary War** (1775–1783), the English Parliament began to impose a series of taxes on the American colonists. Every time the colonists bought certain goods, such as paper products and tea, they had to pay a tax. But the colonists had no representation in Parliament to protest such taxes.

In response to these kinds of actions, **colonial** leader John Adams wrote an essay that was published in 1765. He wrote, "Let it be known that British liberties are not the grants [given by] of princes or parliaments…that many of our rights are inherent and essential [part of every man]."

Colonists protest

On December 16, 1773, in an event known as the Boston Tea Party, angry colonists dumped a shipment of tea into Boston Harbor. They did this to express their anger over an unfair tax on tea. As punishment, Parliament closed the port of Boston. This would limit the colonies' ability to trade.

John Adams became the first vice president and the second president of the United States.

December 16, 1773
In the Boston Tea Party, American colonists protest taxes on tea by throwing a shipment of tea into Boston Harbor.

During the Boston Tea Party, men dumped tea overboard to protest the taxes on it.

"No [taxes] may be levied [imposed] in our kingdom without its general consent…"

—*Magna Carta*

In 1774 colonial leader Thomas Jefferson wrote that Parliament had taken away "rights which God and the laws have given equally and independently to all." The American colonists increasingly believed they were being denied their rights as free Englishmen—rights guaranteed by the Magna Carta (see boxes to right).

"…we will and grant that all other cities… shall have all their liberties and free customs [trade].

—*Magna Carta*

1774
As punishment for the Boston Tea Party, the British Parliament closes the port of Boston.

The Virginia Declaration of Rights

In April 1775, American colonists and British troops exchanged fire in the towns of Lexington and Concord, in Massachusetts Colony. The Revolutionary War had begun.

As the colonists prepared for independence, a man named George Mason wrote a document called the Virginia Declaration of Rights. In this document, he proposed that "all men are by nature equally free and independent." He said that government is for the benefit of the people, and that the real power belongs to the people. He added that people have freedom of religion, freedom from unjust imprisonment, and a right to trial by jury. Many of these ideas found their inspiration in the Magna Carta.

John Hancock, leader of the Continental Congress, signs the Declaration of Independence.

April 1775
The battles at Lexington and Concord begin the Revolutionary War.

1776
George Mason writes the Virginia Declaration of Rights.

The Declaration of Independence

In 1776 representatives from the colonies met at an event called the Continental Congress. They discussed the situation between the American colonies and England. The colonists decided it was time to stand up for their rights. A committee of five men was chosen to write a document. Thomas Jefferson composed most of what would become known as the **Declaration of Independence**.

In this declaration, Jefferson used ideas from the Magna Carta, from English **common law**, and from the Virginia Declaration of Rights. On July 4, 1776, the members of the Continental Congress signed the Declaration of Independence.

Thomas Jefferson later became the third U.S. president.

"We hold these truths to be self-evident, that all men are created equal, that they are endowed by their Creator with certain unalienable [impossible to take away] Rights, that among these are Life, Liberty and the pursuit of Happiness."

—*Declaration of Independence*

1776
Thomas Jefferson uses the ideas of the Magna Carta when he writes the Declaration of Independence.

New country, new government

The British army surrendered to the colonists at Yorktown, Virginia, in 1781. The United States would now be a free, independent country.

In 1787 colonial leaders met to write the U.S. **Constitution**. This focused on how the new government would be run. Like the Magna Carta, this would be the supreme law of the land. The beginning words of the Constitution are: "We the people of the United States…" The power would lie with the people.

Bill of Rights

Many Americans agreed about the importance of the Constitution. But they were concerned that it did not protect individual rights. Now that they had their own country, they did not want the new government powerful enough to take away their rights.

This paining shows the Founding Fathers signing the United States Constitution.

October 1781
The Revolutionary War ends when British forces surrender at Yorktown.

June 1788
The Constitution becomes law. It guarantees many of the same liberties given by the Magna Carta.

To solve this problem, many people argued in favor of adding a **bill of rights**. This would protect the rights of individuals, such as the freedom of religion, speech, and a fair trial. It would also prevent a leader from becoming too powerful. In 1791 the Bill of Rights became law.

This chart shows some of the ways the Constitution and its Bill of Rights were inspired by the Magna Carta.

Magna Carta Inspiration	U.S. Interpretation
"…the **barons** shall choose any twenty-five barons…to observe, maintain and cause to be observed the peace and liberties…" —Magna Carta	"All legislative [law-making] powers herein granted shall be vested [in control of] in a Congress of the United States…" —U.S. Constitution (**Article** 1, Section 1)
"…that the English church shall be free…" —Magna Carta	"Congress shall make no law respecting an establishment of religion, or prohibiting the free exercise thereof…" —Bill of Rights (First Amendment)
"No sheriff or bailiff of ours… is to take horses or carts of any free man…without his agreement." —Magna Carta	"…nor be deprived of life, liberty, or property, without due process of law; nor shall private property be taken for public use, without just compensation." —Bill of Rights (Fifth Amendment)

December 15, 1791
The Bill of Rights becomes law. It also guarantees many of the same liberties given by the Magna Carta.

Preserving Ancient Documents

Four original copies of the 1215 Magna Carta survive. One is in Lincoln, England. Another is in Salisbury, England. Two copies are in the Magna Carta Room of the British Library in London.

Magna Carta in the United States

In 1976 the British government loaned one copy of the Magna Carta to the United States, in honor of the country's bicentennial (200th anniversary) celebration. People could view the Magna Carta in a case at the U.S. Capitol. The case was trimmed with gold and showed the seal of King John and other symbols of England. More than five million people saw this copy of the Magna Carta while it was in the United States.

Know It!

Robert Cotton, a leading book collector of the time, once owned both of the copies of the Magna Carta that are now in the British Library. In 1731 a fire broke out in the building where Cotton's manuscripts were stored. One of the Magna Carta copies was damaged.

Once that copy was returned to England, a replica (copy) was displayed in the U.S. Capitol, in Washington, D.C. The **Latin** words from the time of King John and the **barons** can still be seen inside the fancy gold-trimmed case.

In 2010 **archivists** for the U.S. Capitol removed the display case and stone pedestal so they could be preserved. After six weeks, the display was put back in the Capitol, near statues of people who are associated with the **Declaration of Independence**. This arrangement is meant to honor the influence the Magna Carta had on this and other founding documents of the United States.

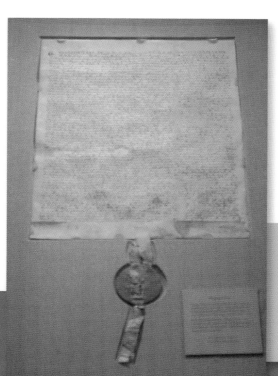

The Magna Carta is displayed in the U.S. Capitol.

Another copy of the Magna Carta

In 1297 King Edward I was forced to once again lay out the terms of the Magna Carta. A copy of this document is on loan to the National Archives in Washington, D.C. A man named David Rubenstein bought it in 2007 for $21.3 million, and he loaned it to the National Archives. He wanted the document to be seen by all U.S. citizens.

An archivist prepares a copy of the Magna Carta for restoration.

2010
The copy of the Magna Carta at the National Archives is restored and preserved.

Restored

In 2010 this copy of the Magna Carta was taken off display so that the **parchment** and ink could be restored. The parchment of the Magna Carta and the ink were carefully examined to see if they needed repair. A new case was built that can protect the Magna Carta copy from humidity (moisture in the air), light, and temperature extremes. Its digital display allows viewers to translate the Latin words of the Magna Carta into English.

The National Archives also has displays of the Declaration of Independence, the **Constitution**, and the **Bill of Rights**. This collection allows a visitor to see the greatest documents that led to the rights of all people in the United States.

"My goal from the outset has been to make this milestone in the historic struggle for freedom available to the American people, now and in the future.... [We have the opportunity] to let the public gain a greater understanding of the intellectual context of the Magna Carta."

—*David Rubenstein, upon loaning the Magna Carta to the National Archives*

Other countries' constitutions

Other countries, such as Australia and Canada, have based their constitutions on the Magna Carta. Australia has a 1297 copy of the Magna Carta preserved and displayed in its **Parliament**.

Human rights

The United Nations (UN) is a group made up of representatives from countries around the world. They work together to solve international problems. In 1948 the UN adopted the Universal Declaration of Human Rights. The goal was to make all governments see that these rights belong to people and should not be taken away. Eleanor Roosevelt, wife of U.S. president Franklin D. Roosevelt, said it "may well become the international Magna Carta of all men everywhere."

The United Nations champions human rights.

Rights for all people

The Magna Carta established that all people, even kings, are not above the law, and that people have rights that cannot be taken away. Even though the Magna Carta was focused on the rights of the barons and not the common people, today people around the world are willing to fight for their rights.

Because of the inspiration of the Magna Carta, documents such as the Declaration of Independence and the U.S. Constitution guarantee rights for citizens of the United States. The power of this 800-year-old document continues to be felt today.

A memorial stands at Runnymede where King John sealed the Magna Carta.

Timeline

1100
King Henry I approves the Charter of Liberties.

1154
King Henry II is crowned. He goes on to enact changes that strengthen the property rights of nobles and the powers of judges in courts.

1170
Thomas Becket is murdered. He had questioned whether the Church had to answer to the king.

1214–1215
King John and the barons fight battles against each other's forces.

1214
The barons gather to discuss the high taxes that King John has imposed.

1213
The pope removes the interdict against England.

June 1215
The two sides meet at Runnymede. The Magna Carta is written and sealed.

1215–1216
The forces of King John and the barons fight again.

October 1216
King John dies. Henry III is crowned king.

1225
King Henry III reconfirms the Magna Carta.

April 1775
The battles at Lexington and Concord begin the Revolutionary War.

1774
As punishment for the Boston Tea Party, the British Parliament closes the port of Boston.

December 16, 1773
In the Boston Tea Party, American colonists protest taxes on tea by throwing a shipment of tea into Boston Harbor.

1776
George Mason writes the Virginia Declaration of Rights.

1776
Thomas Jefferson uses the ideas of the Magna Carta when he writes the Declaration of Independence.

October 1781
The Revolutionary War fighting ends when British forces surrender at Yorktown.

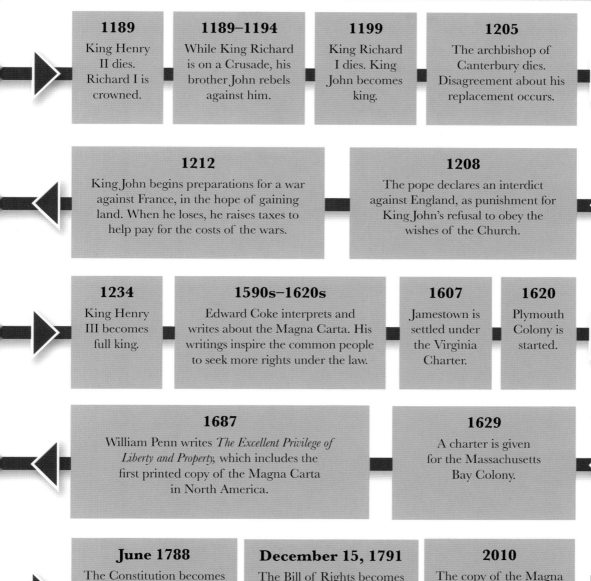

1189
King Henry II dies. Richard I is crowned.

1189–1194
While King Richard is on a Crusade, his brother John rebels against him.

1199
King Richard I dies. King John becomes king.

1205
The archbishop of Canterbury dies. Disagreement about his replacement occurs.

1212
King John begins preparations for a war against France, in the hope of gaining land. When he loses, he raises taxes to help pay for the costs of the wars.

1208
The pope declares an interdict against England, as punishment for King John's refusal to obey the wishes of the Church.

1234
King Henry III becomes full king.

1590s–1620s
Edward Coke interprets and writes about the Magna Carta. His writings inspire the common people to seek more rights under the law.

1607
Jamestown is settled under the Virginia Charter.

1620
Plymouth Colony is started.

1687
William Penn writes *The Excellent Privilege of Liberty and Property*, which includes the first printed copy of the Magna Carta in North America.

1629
A charter is given for the Massachusetts Bay Colony.

June 1788
The Constitution becomes law. It guarantees many of the same liberties given by the Magna Carta.

December 15, 1791
The Bill of Rights becomes law. It also guarantees many of the same liberties given by the Magna Carta.

2010
The copy of the Magna Carta at the National Archives is restored and preserved.

Glossary

archbishop one of the highest-ranking officials of the Catholic Church

archivist expert who works in an archive

article section of a document

baron landowner who owed loyalty to the king

bill of rights document that lists the rights and privileges of the people in a nation

bishop high-ranking official of the Catholic Church

charter legal document granting certain rights

Charter of Liberties list of rights that were approved by King Henry I, providing some rights to the nobles of England

clause section or provision of a contract

colonial relating to a colony

colonist person who lives in a colony

colony area controlled by another country

common law basic law of a country

constitution written set of rules by which a government operates

Declaration of Independence document written by Thomas Jefferson in 1776 that proclaims freedom from Great Britain

interdict declaration of the pope that stops most church rites (ceremonies)

knight soldier ready to fight and defend a baron or king

Latin language of ancient Rome and the official language of the Catholic Church

liberty freedom

monk person who is part of a Catholic religious group

noble person in England who had high rank

parchment thin paper-like material

Parliament main lawmaking body of the British government

pope head of the Catholic Church

primary source document or object made in the past that provides information about a certain time

Revolutionary War American colonists' fight for independence from Great Britain from 1775 to 1783

secondary source account written by someone who studied primary sources

serf person who had little freedom and was bound to work the land for a landowner

tyrant person who rules in a harsh manner, using absolute power

Find Out More

Books

Ching, Jacqueline. *Thomas Jefferson*. New York: Dorling Kindersley, 2009.

Harness, Cheryl. *Revolutionary John Adams*. Washington, D.C.:
   National Geographic, 2006.

Langley, Andrew. *Medieval Life*. New York: DK, 2005.

Swain, Gwenyth. *Declaring Freedom*. Minneapolis, Minn.: Lerner, 2004.

Websites

British Library: Treasures in Full—The Magna Carta
www.bl.uk/treasures/magnacarta/index.html
This website explores the British Library display about the Magna Carta.

Milestone Documents
www.milestonedocuments.com/documents/view/magna-carta/text
Read the text of the Magna Carta and find out more information about it at
this website.

National Archives
www.archives.gov/exhibits/featured_documents/magna_carta/
Visit the website of the National Archives to learn more about the Magna Carta
and its effect on U.S. history.

Index